THE ABUNDANCE MENTALITY

*Experience Deeper Relationships and
More Abundant Living*

by

Sean Kouplen and Mick Schovanec

ISBN: 978-1-942451-17-4
eBook: 978-1-942451-18-1

Published by
Yorkshire Publishing
6271 E. 120th Court
Suite 200
Tulsa, Ok 74137
www.yorkshirepublishing.com

Text Design: Lisa Simpson

Despite having a faith-based leadership focus, distractions are every-where, robbing us of the simple joys of meaningful engagement, critical in enhancing our stakeholder returns. This must-read for any CEO, will capture your heart and keep you in awe, forcing an introspection rarely obtained by reading. Sean and Mick's wisdom is exceptionally communicated. Let the revitalization begin!

Teresa Knox, Owner, Community Care College

Mick and Sean have put together a book that is in direct opposition to the Worlds "I got mine" philosophy. This book will have you thinking thru all our relationships and asking ourselves, Is this an abundant relationship or Is it just for my good. I felt energized and freed as I was reading this book to make my life to not just be about Success or Signifi-cance but to be about Surrender. Surrendering to the greater good to all in HIS kingdom. Thanks for the great read!

Cody Newton, Owner, Mainstream Leadership

Sean and Mick nailed it. They share the secret to "success" in virtually any and every area of your life. And the good news is, you can really achieve it. Regardless of your situation in life, they share how you can achieve success. The path is not easy, but it is simple and it is doable. You owe it to yourself, your family and your friends to read this book.

Stephen R. Frank, President & CEO, OND Financial Services

I truly enjoyed the easy read of your new book "The Abundance Mentality." What a great story to summarize what is said in Philippians 2:3. This book can be a real help to anyone who seems to be getting off track in today's hectic world.

Chuck Woolley, Partner, Kingsley Group

I love this book and the message it brings. Most people seem like they are on the treadmill of life, going faster and faster, with more work and more activities, but with no joy or happiness or sense of fulfillment. The principles outlined in The Abundance Mentality really speak to me, and I am going to incorporate them in my life.

Craig Johnson, CEO, Tenstreet

What a great story with spot on enduring principles! This book will inspire all readers and motivate you to engage in unconditional relationships!

Todd Rolland, CEO, Summit Financial Group

Congratulations! Your book captures the truth. One has to live this truth to believe it.

Jim Brock, Owner, Brock & Associates

You have done it again with another passionate, real-life personal and professional inspiration. Unlike many other motivational best sellers, The Abundance Mentality recognizes the necessity of balance between family, faith and career while embracing the value of "giving" without expectation. A must read for anyone truly seeking healthy, lasting success and the opportunity to share with others.

Julie Hakman, CEO, AmericanChecked, Inc.

The Abundant Mentality is a great application to leadership. The mindset of how to care for those you are called to lead. On a much more important level this is a great perspective on how to care for others and be more effective as the Church!

Rob Beckley, Owasso Campus Pastor, Lifechurch.
TV & Front man for the band "Pillar"

Sean and Mick have captured the natural extension of God's love for his creation ....For God so love us first that it is easy to extend this precept to others if we allow it to function in our lives. Well done!

Tom Wenrick, Owner, Wenrick Development

Sean and Mick have crafted a powerful yet heartwarming message that serves not only as blueprint, but also as a reminder, of how to live a richer, more fulfilling life. Everyone can benefit from the wisdom contained in its pages, no matter what stage of life you're in.

Alex Eaton, CEO, World Travel Service

The Abundance Mentality is a total game changer. It's completely counter-culture to how mainstream America conducts business and personal affairs today, but that's part of the beauty of this book and its authors' insight. A must-read!

Michael S. Neal, CCE, CCD, HLM
President & CEO
Tulsa Regional Chamber

I love this book — it's a quick read yet well-written and packed with life-changing power! In this short, well-written, packed with power book, Sean and Mick unlock the secret of what abundance truly is all about and give you a clear path to get there. Get it, read it and enjoy its rich benefits!

Tim Redmond, Lead Coach at RedmondGrowth.com

Each of us touch lives every day in ways we may never realize. In The Abundance Mentality, intentionality magnifies the power of touch. People are worth the investment.

Travis Jones, Owner, Career Development Partners

So, I thought I had 10 minutes to spare before my next patient, I would just glance through this abundant mentality book. My life will never be the same. I could not put the book down. Amazing life lessons of putting the other persons best interests first. Thank you for this great encouragement. I am excited to build this relationships, as I go take care of my next patient.

Dr.Raj Patel, D.D.S.

What a great message! I don't practice this enough, but really try to for those people who are close to me. This book has inspired me to expand my target group!

Jerry Smith, Owner, Office Everything
and Grove Electric

CONTENTS

FOREWORD
By Jim Stovall

As a result of my 30-plus books—six of them having been made into movies—my arena speeches, television work, national radio program, and my weekly syndicated columns, I have the privilege of communicating with countless people around the world regarding success, happiness, and wealth.

It seems that in our society, everyone wants to "make" more money. The only people who "make" money work at the mint and print our currency. The rest of us have to "earn" money, and the only way we can earn money is to create value in the lives of other people. Misguided individuals who want to have more money without being willing to create value are like the poor soul standing in front of the fireplace imploring it to give him some heat, and then he will throw in some wood.

There are universal laws that have been put in place since the beginning of time involving supply and demand, harvesting and reaping, poverty and wealth. In this book my friend and colleague Sean Kouplen and Mick Schovanec will guide you through these core principles that can take you from where you are to where you want to be.

Money is never a goal. It is a tool that helps us reach our goals. Money gives us choices. Wealth in the hands of generous, giving, and well-adjusted people can make the world a better place. Wealth in the hands of self-serving and narrow-minded people can create chaos and destruction.

There are few people who will ever read this book who have been as poor as I have been and still fewer who have enjoyed as much wealth as I currently have. All things being equal, having money is better than not having money. Nothing can take the place of money in the things it does, but money alone will not make you happy, healthy, or satisfied.

As you read *The Abundance Mentality*, keep in mind that it is, indeed, a state of mind and not a financial condition. If you took all the money in the world and divided it equally among everyone, in a few short years, the wealth would be back in the hands of the people who hold it today. Knowledge, attitude, and principles are the key to wealth. Lottery winners, athletes with million-dollar signing bonuses, and people who inherit huge fortunes without the stability to manage it are often broke and farther in debt in a few short years.

Sean and Mick will give you the mentality to manage money and, more importantly, manage yourself as a person of wealth.

I'm looking forward to your success and your prosperity.

Jim Stovall

2015

PREFACE

Therefore I tell you, do not worry about your life, what you will eat or drink; or about your body, what you will wear. Is not life more than food, and the body more than clothes? Look at the birds of the air; they do not sow or reap or store away in barns, and yet your heavenly Father feeds them. Are you not much more valuable than they? Can any one of you by worrying add a single hour to your life?

And why do you worry about clothes? See how the flowers of the field grow. They do not labor or spin. Yet I tell you that not even Solomon in all his splendor was dressed like one of these. If that is how God clothes the grass of the field, which is here today and tomorrow is thrown into the fire, will he not much more clothe you— you of little faith?

So do not worry, saying, 'What shall we eat?' or 'What shall we drink?' or 'What shall we wear? For the pagans run after all these things, and your heavenly Father knows that you need them. But seek first his kingdom and his righteousness, and all these things will be given to you as well. Therefore do not worry about tomorrow, for tomorrow will worry about itself.

For I was hungry and you gave me food, I was thirsty and you gave me drink, I was a stranger and you welcomed me, I was naked and you clothed me, I was sick and you visited me, I was in prison and you came to me.' Then the righteous will answer him, saying, 'Lord, when did we see you hungry and feed you, or thirsty and give you drink? And when did we see you a stranger and welcome you, or naked and clothe you? And when did we see you sick or in prison and visit you?' And the King will answer them, 'Truly, I say to you, as you did it to one of the least of these my brothers, you did it to me.'

—Jesus of Nazareth, 30 A.D.

CHAPTER 1

FRUSTRATION

CHAPTER 1

≈

FRUSTRATION

Pennsylvania Avenue was bustling with noise on a beautiful summer evening in the Plaza District of Kansas City, Missouri. Couples were holding hands and families were laughing as they walked from shop to shop. Drivers honked as they maneuvered for parking spots in the busy shopping district.

Meanwhile, Bruce Monahan sipped his gin and tonic and tried to unwind after another grueling week of work. Bruce was a financial planner for a well-known firm in town and had just celebrated his eighth anniversary.

Unfortunately, he was afraid this would be his last. His clientele continued to dwindle and so did his income. He didn't have any close relationships at work and his personal life was a mess.

Bruce and Jenny, his wife of fourteen years, divorced a little over a year ago and they no longer spoke to each other. His children rarely came to visit him and, when they did, it seemed awkward and forced.

Bruce didn't have any close friends outside of work to speak of. His buddies from high school and college never reached out to him. He almost felt invisible.

As Bruce sipped on his drink, he just couldn't understand where he went wrong.

How did he get here?

CHAPTER 2

THE BACKSTORY

THE BACKSTORY

Bruce Monahan grew up in Overland Park, a suburb of Kansas City, in an upper middle class home. His father was a successful banker and his mother took care of Bruce and his two sisters.

Bruce was the middle child and always worked hard to please his parents. He made good grades in high school, was popular with his classmates, and became a starter on the varsity baseball team.

When he graduated from high school, he attended the University of Kansas and joined a fraternity. He did well in school and graduated with honors. A fraternity connection helped him land his first job with one of Kansas City's largest investment brokerage firms.

Bruce met Jenny right after graduation. They met on a blind date set up by her college roommate. They fell in love and were married eighteen months later. They had three beautiful children and were very happy.

As Bruce's financial planning clientele grew, so did his social standing and the demands of his job. He joined a local country club and bought a new full-size SUV. He moved the family into a more expensive neighborhood and the kids attended a private school.

Things started to become tighter financially so he worked longer hours to make more money. This hurt his relationship with Jenny and she became frustrated. He began to feel attacked and unappreciated, and started finding reasons not to come home. Ultimately, they grew apart and decided to file for divorce.

Bruce lost focus at work and began to lose clients. He was shocked that some of his strongest client relationships could leave him so easily. Years of hard work and great performance would dissipate with one underperforming quarter.

The stress of his life began to take its toll on him and he became depressed. His life was certainly not turning out the way he had planned.

CHAPTER 3

THE STRANGER

CHAPTER 3

⤳

THE STRANGER

As he stared out the window of his favorite restaurant, Bruce felt someone sit down at the bar beside him. He glanced to his right and noticed an elderly gentleman ordering a club soda.

Bruce was in no mood to talk, but the gentleman didn't seem to notice.

"Tough week of work son?"

"Tough year of work."

"I'm sorry to hear that. My name is George." The elderly gentleman stuck his hand out.

"I'm Bruce." Bruce shook his hand and didn't want to be rude, but he really wasn't interested in entertaining a senior citizen this evening.

George continued. "I know it's none of my business, but you're in a tough stage of life, Bruce. I remember trying to balance work and family at your age. It was one of the most challenging times of my life. How old are you, late thirties?"

"Thirty-seven." Bruce appreciated George's concern; he was just embarrassed that his pathetic life was so obvious to others.

"It will get better, Bruce. Just hang in there."

"I'm trying to 'hang in there,' George, but things just don't seem to be going very well for me right now." Bruce wasn't sure exactly why he felt the need to share with George, but he did.

"Tell me about your situation, Bruce. Maybe I can help."

Bruce was typically very uncomfortable sharing personal details with a complete stranger, but for some reason felt at ease talking with George. He told George about his challenges at work and in his personal life.

George never interrupted him and listened intently. Bruce could not remember the last time someone listened to him like this. Almost an hour had gone by and George had only asked an occasional question or acknowledged Bruce's challenging circumstances.

Bruce finally apologized. "George, I'm sorry I'm talking your ear off. I don't know what has come over me. You are just so easy to talk to."

George told Bruce that he could completely relate to his situation. He remembered being in the same spot thirty years ago. His business and marriage were suffering and he felt lost, but he received some advice that changed his life.

"Unfortunately, I don't have time to share it with you now, Bruce. I have to meet my family across the street for dinner, but if you will call me on Monday, we can continue our conversation." George handed Bruce a business card and made his way out of the crowded bar.

"That would be great, George. I'll call you tomorrow!"

Bruce looked down at the business card. It read: George Patterson, Chairman of the Board, Patterson Industries.

Bruce had just been talking with one of the most successful businessmen in town.

CHAPTER 4

KANSAS CITY'S RICHEST MAN

Chapter 4

~

Kansas City's Richest Man

George was a legend in the Kansas City business and philanthropic communities. Dubbed by the local press as "Kansas City's Warren Buffet," George was a self-made billionaire who was now Missouri's wealthiest man. He owned business interests in finance, manufacturing, energy, and agriculture. Everything he touched seemed to turn to gold.

Remarkably, George Patterson started out with nothing. His father and grandfather were both sharecroppers and George worked right alongside them. He put himself through college and started on the ground floor of a local bank. He was promoted quickly through the ranks to become the youngest chairman in the bank's history, and he began to carefully diversify his investments and create substantial wealth.

The most amazing fact about George Patterson, however, is that he did not sacrifice his family to achieve his financial goals. He is still married to Mary, his wife of fifty-two years. His three children are all successful and well adjusted. Business leaders throughout the state boasted about his kindness and compassion. By all indications, he had lived an abundant life.

Bruce couldn't believe that Kansas City's most successful businessman was so interested in his story. Didn't he have more important things to do than listen to some washed up financial planner talk about his problems?

Regardless, the conversation was therapeutic for Bruce and made him feel so much better. He couldn't wait to continue their discussion and hoped that George was sincere in wanting to meet with him again.

On Monday morning, Bruce called George's office and spoke with his executive assistant Dianne. George had already told Dianne to expect Bruce's call and she immediately set an appointment for them after work on Thursday evening at the same restaurant where they first met.

CHAPTER 5

BUILDING THE FOUNDATION

CHAPTER 5

⌁

BUILDING THE FOUNDATION

Bruce arrived at the restaurant early and waited for George. He had been anxiously waiting for their meeting all day.

At exactly 6 p.m., George walked in and gave Bruce a warm handshake and pat on the shoulder. "I have been looking forward to getting to know you better, Bruce."

"Me too, George! Thank you so much for taking the time to visit with me."

The two men enjoyed small talk, ordered dinner and continued their discussion. "So Bruce, where do you think things went wrong?" George was very direct, but spoke in such a kind tone that Bruce didn't mind.

"I don't know, George. I think I just got caught up in financial success and wanted to keep up with clients and friends. I should have been more careful and kept my standard of living lower."

"There is no question that outliving our means is a dangerous habit, but why do you suppose your business and personal relationships all dried up?"

"I think people are just selfish. They only want to be your friend or client as long as you can bring them value. When you can't, they toss you to the curb."

George smiled. He remembered feeling the same when he was about Bruce's age. "Bruce, I really don't think that's your problem."

"What do you mean?"

"Bruce, I promised my wife I would be home by 7:30 p.m., but I want to give you a homework assignment."

A homework assignment? Bruce was skeptical, but he was also desperate. "Okay, what is it?"

"Bruce, I want you to think about the people you like to be around and do business with. What is the one thing they all have in common? Please think about that and I'll see you here, same time next week."

CHAPTER 6

THE ONE THING

CHAPTER 6

THE ONE THING

Bruce spent hours thinking about the people he most liked to be around and do business with, but he struggled to come up with something they had in common.

His favorite friends and business associates were all so different. They were all different ages, races, and religions. Some were well educated and some weren't. Some came from upper class families while some grew up very poor. Some were successful financially and some weren't. They didn't seem to have anything in common.

As he sat at the restaurant and waited for George to arrive, he just could not figure out the answer to George's homework assignment.

George sat down and ordered his customary club soda. "So, did you come up with the answer to my homework assignment, Bruce?"

"I just don't know, George. I'm sorry, but my best friends and business relationships are all so different."

George laughed. "Bruce, I am confident that all of your favorite people have one thing in common."

"What is it?"

"How do they make you feel?"

"How do they make me feel? What do you mean, George?"

"Think about all of the people you love and enjoy the most. How do they make you feel?"

Bruce had never thought about this before. He began to think about his parents, his best friends from high school and college, his favorite clients, and other people that he loved being around.

"I've never thought about it before, but I guess every one of those people care about me and make me feel special."

"Bingo! That is exactly the right answer, Bruce. All of us want to be around people who care about us."

Bruce knew from studying George's background that he was a very caring person, but he couldn't quite understand what this had to do with his problems.

"Obviously we all want to be loved and cared for George, but I don't quite understand how this is going to help me. Clearly, I am not feeling very loved or cared for at the moment."

"Bruce, there are millions of people just like you throughout our country. We have hundreds of friends on Facebook, but no one to call when we need to talk or need a helping hand. We are constantly in a hurry and don't even know our neighbors or coworkers. Our relationships are so shallow because we don't take the time to get to know each other.

"We are all so busy trying to make ends meet that we have forgotten the fabric of life. We simply focus on 'what's in it for us' without building lasting relationships that will stand with us through thick and thin."

Bruce sat quietly for a moment and absorbed what George had just said. It was as if George had known his entire story.

"George, it's sad, but the life you just described is mine. I have no real friends, my wife has left me, and my clients left me as soon as there was a downturn in the market. I feel completely empty inside and I just don't know what to do."

"I know exactly how you feel, Bruce. I felt that way when I was younger, but I learned there is a better way to live. Unfortunately, we are out of time. I will share what I learned with you next week. Okay?"

"Absolutely, George. Same time and same place?"

"Yes, sir. See you then. Have a great week!"

CHAPTER 7

THE ABUNDANCE MENTALITY

CHAPTER 7

⁀

THE ABUNDANCE MENTALITY

B ruce began to feel a sense of optimism for the first time in years. He wasn't sure how George's discussion about being caring was going to turn his situation around, but he was very excited to continue learning from him.

At 6 p.m. sharp, George showed up at the table and ordered a club soda. "Hello, Bruce! How was your day?"

Somehow, Bruce got the feeling that George really meant it when he asked him about his day. "It was a little rough, George. I lost another large client today, but I am hopeful that my luck is going to change."

"It's not a matter of luck, Bruce. Today, I want to share with you the secret to an abundant life and career."

"I need a secret, George. What I am doing is clearly not working very well."

"Bruce, I was raised very poor and my family always seemed to fight over money. As I grew older, I began to realize that this constant focus on money really had a negative impact on me.

"When I became your age, I viewed life from a scarcity mentality."

"What is a scarcity mentality, George?"

"I lived in fear and felt like there was never enough. In my mind, Mary and I never had enough money, no matter how much we saved. I never had enough job security and I was scared of being fired at any time. I never felt like I had enough clients and I was constantly afraid that I would lose them. I lived in a perpetual state of fear that I wasn't good enough and my life was going to fall apart at any moment."

"I know that feeling. It is miserable."

"It was. I spent every day wondering when the other shoe was going to drop."

"So what changed?"

"For years, I had been praying for happiness and contentment. Then, three things happened in the same month that helped me begin to change my way of thinking.

"First, I read *Seven Habits of Highly Effective People* by Stephen Covey and he discussed a concept called the abundance mentality.

"Second, I attended a men's bible study group, in which we discussed the topic of abundance within the Bible. We reviewed multiple verses in which Jesus assures us that we should not worry and He will take care of us.

"Finally, I was at a conference with a banker friend of mine and we were visiting between seminars. I was lamenting about how competitive our industry was and I asked him if our banks were going to survive. He smiled and encouraged me to maintain an abundance mentality instead of a scarcity mentality. I began to think that there must be something to this abundance mentality concept!"

"What is an abundance mentality, George?"

"Bruce, the word abundance is a wonderful word. It means overflowing fullness or over-sufficient supply. Can you imagine having overflowing fullness in resources, relationships, love, and joy? Wouldn't that be a wonderful way to live?"

"Absolutely. That sounds like heaven!"

"It sure does, Bruce. An abundance mentality is a state of believing there is abundance to meet all of your needs. You realize there is plenty for everyone and you do not have to spend all of your time worrying about provision."

"Wow, I have never felt this way George. I have always been scared that there would not be enough for my family and me, and I have contributed to this issue by increasing my standard of living. This abundance mentality mindset makes life feel so easy and effortless. My life has always seemed like such a struggle."

"I would encourage you to read what the Bible says about abundance, Bruce. Spend some time praying that God would change your thinking from a scarcity mentality to an abundance mentality."

"I sure will, George."

"Bruce, I better head home, but please focus on developing an abundance mentality until we meet next week."

CHAPTER 8

ABUNDANT RELATIONSHIPS

CHAPTER 8

~

ABUNDANT RELATIONSHIPS

B ruce thought a lot about maintaining an abundance mentality. Every night, he would meditate and pray on scriptures such as Ephesians 3:20, John 10:10, Malachi 3:10, Matthew 6:25-26, Matthew 6:33, and others that discussed abundance. He was shocked at how often Jesus discussed abundance in the Bible!

He also prayed continuously that God would help to change his mindset from one of scarcity to abundance. He began to feel a difference in the way he approached life. He started to believe that there were plenty of resources for him and he didn't have to be afraid.

Thursday evening came around and George arrived punctually at 6 p.m., as usual. "Bruce, have you been thinking about abundance?"

"Yes, sir, I have."

"Have you had any revelations?"

"I am starting to feel better, George. I certainly like the idea that there is plenty for everyone and I obviously believe what Jesus tells us, so I am becoming more optimistic."

"That's great, Bruce. Now, I want to tell you why having an abundance mentality is so important."

"Sounds great."

"Bruce, I don't believe we were meant to rush through life taking what we can get and simply surviving. I believe we were meant to have abundant relationships with others, but we can't do this unless we have an abundance mentality."

"What do you mean by abundant relationships, George?"

"Unfortunately, we have become a society that is in it for ourselves. We are very selfish. On a global scale, greed and scandal have become the norm rather than the exception. We will do whatever it takes to get ahead and get the result that we want.

"It's even worse on a personal scale. We only think about ourselves, about our own needs. Just think about it, Bruce—when was the last time you really thought about the well-being of someone else?"

Bruce had learned that George never asked a question without having a good reason for it, so he really thought about his answer. The result wasn't good.

"George, I hate to admit this, but I honestly can't remember the last time I thought about the well-being of someone else. I have been so focused on my own problems and issues that I never really think about the needs of others."

"You aren't alone, Bruce. Selfishness is an epidemic within our society. No one thinks about others anymore. Our lives are too complex and move too fast to care about others. The good news is that you and I have the power to change this through a concept I call abundant relationships."

"How do abundant relationships work?"

"Bruce, abundant relationships are very countercultural. In an abundant relationship, we always look out for the other person's best interest, even if it does not benefit us, and we help the other person with nothing expected in return."

"Wow, you are really talking about selfless living."

"This is just a completely different way of approaching relationships and it will change your life for the better. I was a little older than you when I learned this amazing secret to life.

"I was working long, hard hours trying to get ahead and looking for any angle that I could find to make a buck. Then, one day, I met a gentleman named Nick Parker at a local networking event. We went to lunch together and he was one of the nicest people I had ever met. He was so genuine and caring, and he really listened to what I had to say.

"Ironically, he was a financial planner just like you and I kept waiting for him to shake me down for all of my insurance and investment business, but he never did. I knew what he did for a living, but he never forced it on me. He was 100 percent interested in the well-being of me and my family."

"Wow! I have never met anyone like that."

"Neither had I. Until then, every person in my life, except for my immediate family, had some type of motive or angle. They all wanted something from me and, if I couldn't help them get what they wanted, our relationship was expendable. I just thought that was how life worked until I met Nick. He changed my life."

"That is amazing, George. Is that why you are so successful today?"

"I really think it is, Bruce. I began trying to live my life like Nick and it has paid tremendous dividends over the years."

Bruce let George's comments soak in. George's advice was so simple, yet so profound. He just didn't know how he could get there from his current situation.

"George, I love this idea of abundant relationships, but I have been so selfish for so long. I don't think anyone will believe that the 'new me' is now genuinely interested in their well-being. How do I achieve this?"

"Bruce, unfortunately, we are out of time for tonight, but I will give you the steps to building abundant relationships next week when we meet. Fair enough?"

"Absolutely."

Bruce sat in silence for a moment.

"George, there's just one thing I don't understand."

"What's that, Bruce?"

"Why are you doing this for me?"

"You'll find out next time."

Chapter 9

One Step at a Time

CHAPTER 9

⌒

ONE STEP AT A TIME

Bruce thought about abundant relationships all week until his next meeting with George. Day by day, he did his best to focus on other people's needs instead of his own. He noticed that other people's attitudes toward him slowly seemed to become more positive, and he was starting to feel better about himself.

He was sitting at their table thinking about how he could develop abundant relationships throughout all areas of his life when George walked up.

"Good evening, Bruce! Have you been thinking about the concept of abundant relationships?"

"I sure have, George. I have been trying to build abundant relationships at work and I am really starting to see a difference. It is exciting, but it seems overwhelming to build abundant relationships in all areas of my life."

"I felt the same way, Bruce, but over time it just becomes who you are. I do think there are a few key steps to remember as you begin developing abundant relationships in all areas of your life."

"What are they, George?" Bruce pulled out a notepad and started taking notes.

"Bruce, as we have discussed, to build abundant relationships, you must first develop an abundance mentality. If you truly believe there is enough for everyone, your relationships can focus more on the person and less on what you need to gain from them."

"I've been working on that, George."

"Great. Next, we must genuinely care about the person we are building a relationship with. Whether we are dealing with our spouse, children, coworkers, clients, or friends, we must value them as people and not as a means to an end. We must care about them and their wants, needs, and challenges."

"How can I do this, George?"

"Bruce, I always try to picture the love that Jesus has for me. I am far from perfect and have made huge mistakes in my life, but he loves me anyway. He doesn't love me because of what I can offer him, and I should look at the people in my life the same way. If we can genuinely care about the people in our life, even those that we don't particularly like, it will make it much easier to focus on helping them and not 'selling' to them."

"That makes perfect sense. What's the next step, George?"

"Next, we must learn to listen. Not pretend to listen while we determine what we will say next, but really listen intently to what people are saying and how they are feeling. Do you remember what it felt like when we first met and I just listened to you?"

"Yes, it felt amazing!"

"That is how others will feel if you will listen to them without interrupting or talking over them. Listening also allows us to meet the other person's needs instead of making our assumptions about what they need."

"That's a great one. Then what?"

"The fourth step is the most important. Once we have listened intently to their needs, we must help the other person to the best of our ability, even if there is no benefit to us."

"That seems easy, George."

"Quite the opposite, Bruce. Just think about what this means. My wife might need help with the household chores, but I really dislike doing them. My client might need a product or service that I cannot provide, but I don't want them to go to a competitor. My children might need help with their homework, but I just don't have time. Or, my coworker might need help with an assignment that, if successful, could get them promoted over me."

"Oh, wow. I take back what I said. Those are very difficult situations."

"They are, but to create abundant relationships, we must *always* do what is right for the other person."

"So this is why you spend time with me, right George? There is no benefit to you, but you listened carefully to me and you are helping me meet a need."

"That is correct. Plus, I also happen to think you're a pretty neat guy."

"That is amazing. I've never seen anyone live this way."

"I had never seen it either until I witnessed my friend Nick. I literally watched him call a large client of his, who had just awarded him a huge amount of business, for the sole purpose of telling them that he was not the best provider in the industry for the product. He told them they should go with his primary competitor!"

"Are you serious?"

"Yes, he risked a five figure commission by being honorable. Fortunately, the client admired his integrity so much, that he awarded Nick this business as well as additional business! Now, it doesn't always work out that way, but we must always do what's in the best interest of the other party."

"Wow. Any other steps?"

"Bruce, our final step is to learn to receive the blessings from this type of living."

"What do you mean, George?"

"Over time, your relationships will grow deeper and people will want to bless you in business or personally. Perhaps they will refer friends and family to you, or they might give you unexpected gifts or do certain favors for you. You must learn to receive these blessings properly."

"What do you mean by receiving them properly?"

"If they are personal favors or gifts, you must just learn to be gracious and accept them. Do not resist them. So often, we feel unworthy or guilty when great things happen to us, but we must remember that Jesus wants us to have an abundant life and provides us with wonderful blessings. We should not push blessings away."

"Is it different with business?"

"Yes, this is more difficult. You will find over time that, as your relationships deepen, many people will want to do business with you and refer their friends and family to you. You must be prepared to handle this new business efficiently or they cannot continue referring business to you.

"Dan Sullivan with Strategic Coach calls this dynamic being 'referable' and he discusses 'Four Referability Habits' in his book *How the Best Get Better*. These habits are: Show up on time, do what you say you will do, finish what you start, and say please and thank you. If you have abundant relationships and practice these four habits, you will experience tremendous growth and prosperity like you have never seen."

"Those four habits should be pretty easy to follow."

"They are not as easy to follow as you might think, Bruce. Early on, when you have a small number of abundant relationships and minimal business, it's very easy. Later, when you have a very large number of relationships and a huge amount of business, it becomes very difficult. We must always evaluate our processes and procedures to make sure we handle new business efficiently.

"Let me give you an example. I have another very good friend who is in the insurance business. He is kind, caring, and intelligent, and he has a huge portfolio of clients. I try to refer him business, but he is so busy that he never calls them back and they always have a bad experience. I can no longer refer business to him, even though we have an abundant relationship."

Bruce looked at his watch and knew it was time for George to go. "Thank you George. Now I understand what you mean by receiving the blessings properly."

George smiled. "You're welcome. I'll see you next week, Bruce!"

CHAPTER 10

THE ABUNDANCE
MENTALITY IN ACTION

CHAPTER 10

~

THE ABUNDANCE MENTALITY IN ACTION

Bruce was blown away by the concept of abundant relationships and really studied the steps that George had shared with him. It changed the way he thought about his relationships and the people in his life.

He was thinking about how selfish he had been when George joined him for their next weekly meeting. "Good evening Bruce, how was your day?"

"Things really seem to be improving, George. I'm so grateful to you for spending so much time with me."

"I enjoy it just as much as you do, my friend! We are coming to the end of our 'formal' time together, but I would like to spend our last couple of meetings talking about how to put the abundance mentality and abundant relationships into practice."

"That sounds great!"

"Bruce, it's important to note that society will continuously push you away from your abundance mentality. The media will constantly tell you how bad everything is and make you feel like you are going to lose everything. Certain friends and business associates will approach your relationship with motives and selfishness. Occasionally, even people that you share an abundant relationship with will disappoint you. You must rise above this and remain consistent. Over time, you will see an amazing difference in the quality of your life."

"I know it won't be easy, George. I am sure people have disappointed you in the past. How have you managed to live this way for so long?"

"First and foremost, I enjoy it. Living with an abundance mentality has really elevated my life to a higher level than just trying to accumulate assets and wealth. This becomes very empty over time.

"I also try to remember that living this way has significant benefits for me personally. Studies show that people who live this way have less stress in their lives and live longer than others. Interestingly, when we help someone else with no selfish intentions, our bodies emit a hormone that makes us happy and is very good for our heart. It is very similar to the hormone that helps mothers endure childbirth!"

"It's too bad everyone doesn't live this way, isn't it?"

"It really is, Bruce, but we are just conditioned otherwise. Just think about it for a moment. In life today, all we think about is 'what's in it for me?' I need to sell you something so that I will earn money and my needs will be met. I'll scratch your back, but only if you scratch mine.

"With an abundance mentality, I focus on you, not me. I am thinking only about how I can help you, whether it benefits me or not. There is no keeping score in relationships and I don't get upset if you don't reciprocate personally or in business. This type of living is exactly the opposite of what we have been taught."

"I will definitely remember these things, George. I know I will still have tough days ahead."

"We all have tough days, but I am confident that you are going to be very successful, Bruce. I hate to go, but I better run. At our final meeting next week, I want to tell you about the abundance loop."

"That sounds great, George. I'll see you next week!"

CHAPTER 11

THE ABUNDANCE LOOP

THE ABUNDANCE LOOP

Bruce was a little sad as he approached the restaurant for his final weekly meeting with George. He had grown to enjoy these visits so much, and he looked forward to them all week. As he approached their table, he noticed that George was already there and had another gentlemen with him.

"Hi, George! I didn't mean to interrupt. Would you like for me to come back later?"

"Absolutely not, Bruce! We have been waiting for you. I would like to introduce you to Greg Haney."

"Greg Haney. Are you the same Greg Haney that is the mayor of Kansas City?"

"I sure am."

"Wow, what an honor to meet you! George, how did you get the mayor to come spend time with me?"

"Bruce, I felt like it would be very impactful for you to hear Greg's story. You remind me a lot of Greg. His situation was very similar to yours when we first met."

Greg leaned forward in his chair. "Bruce, George took me under his wings about fifteen years ago and changed my life, and I would love to tell you about it."

"I am so honored, Mayor Haney. Please tell me your story."

"Bruce, please call me Greg. I had been languishing in corporate America, struggling to make ends meet, and fighting to save my marriage when a client of mine suggested that I visit with George Patterson. George was much younger then and, while very successful, he certainly wasn't as well known as he is today.

"When we met, I was blown away. I had never met anyone so sincere and caring in my life. George listened intently to me and shared the concept of the abundance mentality and abundant relationships. I began to focus more on others and less on myself. I practiced the steps that George taught me, and it changed my life."

"Wow. Mayor—I mean Greg—I just assumed that you had always been successful and at the top of your game."

"Not at all, Bruce. I was in a very similar position to you when I was your age, but as I developed an abundance mentality and built abundant relationships, my circle of influence really started to grow. My relationships became deeper and I earned a high level of trust with some very successful people here in Kansas City.

"These individuals would introduce me to their friends and family members, and I would always do the right thing for them, even if it did not benefit me. Soon, my abundant relationships grew so large that I was promoted to the head of my company. One day, a couple of my board members told me that our existing mayor was planning to retire and they encouraged me to run for office. I did and the rest is history."

"This all happened in less than fifteen years?"

George jumped in. "It was really only ten years, Bruce. Greg has been in office for almost five years now. This is the power of the abundance mentality and the abundance loop."

Bruce was a little confused. "George, maybe I missed something. What is the abundance loop?"

"That is today's lesson, Bruce. The abundance loop is what Greg has described to you. It occurs when you give selflessly into the lives of others—deeper relationships follow, and these individuals will naturally want to help you. They refer their friends and family to you, you give selflessly into their lives and deeper relationships develop, they refer their friends and family to you ... and the loop continues."

"That is powerful. So, as your number of abundant relationships grows, you naturally become more abundant without even trying."

"That is the abundance loop!"

Bruce was overwhelmed. This was such a powerful concept and he couldn't believe that George Patterson, Kansas City's most influential man, brought Greg Haney, Kansas City's mayor, here just to teach him the power of the abundance loop.

"George, I really don't know how to thank you enough. You have changed my life. How can I repay you?"

"It has been my pleasure, Bruce. You are a very special young man. All I ask is that you pass this information on if you are ever given the chance."

"I certainly will."

Chapter 12

The Rest of the Story

THE REST OF THE STORY

Bruce intentionally practiced The Abundance Mentality every day for the rest of his life, and the results were amazing. He and George stayed in touch and grabbed dinner at their favorite restaurant every few months.

Bruce was able to keep his job as a financial planner and saw his client relationships become much stronger as he put their needs first.

His relationship with his coworkers became stronger as they realized they could trust him to do the right thing and support them. After about five years, he was promoted to Department Head and ultimately, Managing Partner of their firm.

His relationship with his children became stronger as he invested more time with them and started really listening to them and supporting them. He now has three beautiful grandchildren that he sees on a regular basis.

His relationship with his friends strengthened as he began making them a priority and spending more time with them. They were shocked at what a great listener and sincere, caring person he had become. They all take two golf trips per year to stay connected.

Best of all, Bruce apologized to his ex-wife Jenny for the way he had taken her for granted while they were married. They began spending time together and she noticed a drastic difference in him. They became good friends again and ultimately got remarried! They are enjoying life together as grandparents.

George lived to be ninety-three years old and maintained the abundance mentality as long as he lived. His funeral was held in the Kansas City Convention Center and was filled with thousands of family members, close friends and admirers. It was a beautiful ceremony.

Among the speakers at his funeral were Greg Haney, Kansas City's most popular mayor; John Vanderslice, Missouri's current governor; and Bruce Monahan, widely touted as George Patterson's prize pupil. It was the greatest honor of Bruce's life.

Bruce spoke about his experience with George Patterson and what a selfless, giving man he was. He had no idea that the talkative older gentlemen at the bar would ultimately save his life.

After the funeral, a beautiful reception was held in Union Station where friends and family members had an opportunity to share their favorite memories of George. The experience was overwhelming for Bruce as hundreds of people stepped up to the microphone to share what George had done for them.

This was the result of the abundance mentality.

CHAPTER 13

FULL CIRCLE

CHAPTER 13

FULL CIRCLE

Years went by and it was a beautiful June evening in downtown Kansas City. Bruce was wrapping up for the day and stared out the window of his corner office toward the restaurant where he first met George Patterson.

Bruce glanced down at his desk at a faded picture of him and George that was taken the first night they met. He then looked at the beautiful family pictures, plaques, and trophies that lined his shelves. He had been blessed with such a wonderful life.

A tear slowly fell down Bruce's face as he thought about the amazing difference George Patterson made in his life. How could he ever repay him?

Suddenly his phone rang.

"Bruce, this is John Vanderslice. How are you today?"

"Hello, Governor Vanderslice. I was actually just sitting here thinking about our good friend George Patterson. I sure do miss him."

"So do I, Bruce. It's interesting that you would mention George Patterson. His grandson is an excellent young man, but he has hit a bit of a rough spot in life. Do you think you could grab a cup of coffee with him and see if you could help him out? I couldn't think of anyone better than George's prize pupil to get him back on track."

Bruce remembered the commitment he made to his good friend George Patterson many years ago.

"I would be honored to help him, Governor. Please tell him I will meet him at the restaurant across the street at 6 p.m. on Thursday evening."

EXECUTIVE SUMMARY:

HOW TO LIVE THE
ABUNDANCE MENTALITY

1. Change your thinking from a scarcity mentality to an abundance mentality. Start believing there is plenty for everyone and you don't have to constantly worry about provision. This will allow you to develop abundant relationships.

2. Genuinely care about every person you are building a relationship with. Value them as people and not as a means to an end.

3. Learn to listen. Really focus on what the other person is saying and how they are feeling. Do not interrupt them, talk over them, or think about the next things you will say while they are talking.

4. Help the other person to the best of your ability, even if it there is no benefit to you. Be honest if you are not the best solution for his or her problem.

5. Learn to receive the blessings from abundance relationships. Don't feel guilty about the blessings you will receive. Practice the referability habits to continue receiving new business referrals.

AFTERWORD

Your life can change in an instant. Mine took a drastic turn for the better when I grudgingly accepted a meeting request from a man named Mick Schovanec.

Mick sought me out for advice and counsel after hearing about my success and seeing me speak at a couple of local events, but little did I know that accepting that meeting would actually change my life forever.

From the moment Mick stepped into my office, I could sense that there was something drastically different about him. Much like George in our book, Mick is a tremendous listener. He asks great questions and remains fully focused as you talk.

He is a giver. Throughout our relationship, he has never once asked me for anything, but is always seeking to make my life better. His entire approach to our relationship, and others in his life, was something I had rarely seen before. It was so pure and honest with no selfish motive at all.

As our relationship grew, I began to realize this was an amazing way to live life and the principles I learned from Mick were relevant to every relationship in my life. This includes my relationships with my wife, my coworkers, my family, my friends, and my clients.

I began to see tremendous results from this type of living and wanted to share it with the world, and I am so grateful to Mick for joining me to share our story. I realize maintaining an abundance mentality and building abundant relationships is completely countercultural, but I am convinced that this is how life was meant to be lived.

Sean

It was just a short time ago when I met Sean Kouplen at a networking event that he hosts to serve *his* community; I went because I had heard of his generous nature and love for others (the free lunch and speaker were amazing, too.) It is true—when you are around Sean he makes you feel better about yourself. He always has a positive and uplifting attitude accompanied by a large smile and encouraging word. His relationship with friends and business partners around him amaze me. It seems everyone wants a piece of his time.

In the world's eyes "he has made it"—he has an amazing wife and kids, he is Chairman and CEO of a bank he started, and he has successful ownership of many other businesses. You will not find him boasting, as he is always thinking of giving to others. My deep respect and admiration for Sean Kouplen is due to his servant leadership.

Sean eloquently tells stories that are relatable. When you get time around him, you will sense his humility and love and will also want to live life in excellence and with intentional priority.

It wasn't always that way for me. It took me to age forty-three until a major crisis in my life woke me up. Now, we share time together; as the Bible says, "Iron sharpens iron." Sean and I are committed to live the rest of our days on Earth focused on serving others and listening to your stories.

There is a "Sean" in your life waiting to coach and mentor you through good times and bad—someone with "the fruit on the tree" of relationships, personal finance, or whatever area you need help. For me, it is the pursuit of uncomfortably replacing pride with humility and NOT trying to constantly be the provider but being present (listening) to the wisdom that surrounds me and then implementing it in my own life. Have I arrived? NO WAY. Will I live every day on Earth as a "student"? YES. Surrounding yourself with informational truth is the answer.

Thank you, Sean Kouplen, for being George to me!

Mick

PLEASE TELL US YOUR ABUNDANCE MENTALITY STORY!

As The Abundance Mentality has grown in popularity, we have received some amazing stories of people who have given selflessly to others with nothing expected in return.

We heard about Cindy, a carpet salesperson, who told her client that a manufacturer's warranty would help her get her carpet replaced much more inexpensively than buying carpet from Cindy.

We heard about Stephen, the financial planner, who never even asked his client about financial products but rather focused completely on the welfare of him and his family. Stephen also spends hours every week having coffee with other men who need help or advice while he could be selling insurance or investments.

We heard about Frank who quit a great job to lead a ministry for men who are feeling lost.

We heard about business leaders who blessed their employees beyond description, even when their own business was struggling.

We heard about Mark and Carol who helped renovate a friend's house when they were on vacation.

There are SO many great Abundance Mentality stories and we want to hear yours! Please visit our website at www.theabundancementality.net and click on the "Your Abundance Mentality Stories" tab, and tell us your story. You might be in our next book!

Sean and Mick

ABOUT THE AUTHORS

Sean Kouplen is the Chairman & CEO of Regent Bank, a small businesses owner and investor, and a popular author and speaker.

Kouplen has authored two best-selling books including - *Twelve Life Lessons Every Graduate Should Know*, targeted for high school and college graduates; and, *The Priority Promise*, a popular life management book for leaders. The success of his books have led to nationwide speaking engagements to business groups and universities across the country.

On April 1, 2008, Kouplen fulfilled a lifelong dream by leading an investor group that purchased 110-year-old Regent Bank. Since that time, the bank has expanded to Tulsa and OKC, tripling in size from $72 million in assets to $220 million in challenging economic times. Regent Bank has been named the Oklahoma Small Business Financial Services Champion by the Small Business Administration.

Kouplen was the co-founder of Bixby Outreach Center and Bixby Community Church, where he serves as an Elder. He holds numerous local and statewide leadership positions, including OSU-Tulsa Board of Trustees, Tulsa

Chamber Small Business Council, Eastern OK Donated Dental Services, Young President's Organization and Chairman of the Board for OneFire Holding Company—the Creek Nation's business holding company.

Kouplen's many awards include Journal Records Most Outstanding CEO, his fraternity's top national young alumni award, Citizen of the Year in Bixby, and being named to Oklahoma Magazine and Tulsa Business Journal's Top 40 Under 40 lists.

Kouplen has been married to his wife Angela for seventeen years, and they have three children—Emory, Kennedy and Finley.

Mick Schovanec is the owner of a leadership and personal development business, energy company and paintball facility.

Schovanec was raised in a rural farm community in northwest Oklahoma where he learned the principles of hard work and honest character. He loves the sport of baseball and was blessed to play throughout college.

More than two years ago, Schovanec experienced a life-changing event that brought awareness spiritually, mentally and personally. Now he focuses his time on encouraging and affirming others to chase their purpose/calling.

Schovanec was taught through society to be a "provider." He now focuses on being "present," with the daily goal of squashing his pride for humility. He cherishes each moment with his Godly wife Lisa of 21 years, and two children – Logan and Sydnee.

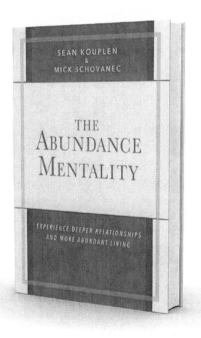

SEAN KOUPLEN
&
MICK SCHOVANEC

THE
ABUNDANCE
MENTALITY

EXPERIENCE DEEPER RELATIONSHIPS
AND MORE ABUNDANT LIVING

Thank you for reading!

Tell Us Your Story

Thank you for taking the time to read The Abundance Mentality. We encourage you to live a life of abundance and we want to hear your story!

Please visit our website at www.theabundancementality.net and click on the "Your Abundance Mentality Stories" tab to share stories about people who have practiced the abundance mentality in your life.

We look forward to hearing your stories and you may be included in our next book!

Speaking Services

Sean Kouplen and Mick Schovanec are sought-after speakers for businesses, educational institutions, youth organizations and church groups throughout the country.

Please email speaker@theabundancementality.net if you are interested in booking either Sean or Mick for your next event.

Our speaking services are reasonably priced and we want to share the abundance mentality message with people throughout the world.

CPSIA information can be obtained at www.ICGtesting.com
Printed in the USA
LVOW11s1353131115

462462LV00001B/9/P

9 781942 451174